Better Ma

Better M

A Bold Reimagining of Robbie Williams' Life in a Satirical Musical Biopic

LINDSEY T. GORDON

COPYRIGHT

TABLE OF CONTENTS

INTRODUCTION

The Genesis of Better Man: Reinterpreting a Pop Icon

The creation of Better Man was as audacious as the life it sought to portray. From its inception, the project was envisioned as more than just a traditional musical biopic.

The idea germinated in 2021 when Michael Gracey, known for his work on The Greatest Showman, sought to explore Robbie Williams' story in a way that captured the raw complexity of his personality and career. Gracey was inspired by Williams' unique blend of humor, vulnerability, and flamboyance, traits that set him apart from other pop icons.

Rather than adhering to the standard tropes of a biographical film, Gracey aimed to craft a narrative that would "reinterpret and recontextualize" the life of Robbie Williams. The film would delve deep into his psyche, exploring themes of identity, self-worth, and resilience.

Gracey's decision to frame the story as a satirical musical not only allowed for creative freedom but also mirrored Robbie's penchant for self-deprecation and irreverence. The result was a bold, multi-layered narrative that spanned three decades of Williams' life, blending heartfelt drama with absurdist humor.

Michael Gracey's Vision: Merging Satire, Music, and Emotion

Gracey's vision for Better Man was to merge satire with the emotional weight of Robbie's life story. The film would oscillate between moments of raw vulnerability and outrageous comedy, echoing the unpredictable nature of Williams himself.

The satirical approach allowed Gracey to push boundaries, addressing heavy topics like addiction, mental health, and fame through a lens that was both empathetic and darkly humorous.

Music played a central role in Gracey's vision. By reinterpreting Robbie's iconic songs to reflect the emotional tone of each scene, the film seamlessly integrated music into its storytelling.

Tracks like Angels and Let Me Entertain You were transformed into powerful narrative tools, conveying Robbie's inner struggles and triumphs. Gracey worked closely with Robbie and his team to ensure the songs captured the essence of the story while staying true to the original spirit of the music.

The film also embraced surrealist elements to depict Robbie's internal battles. Hallucinations, symbolic sequences, and the portrayal of Robbie as a CGI chimpanzee added layers of depth to the narrative. These creative choices reflected the fragmented nature of Robbie's psyche, offering viewers a glimpse into the chaos and beauty of his world.

The Bold Choice: A CGI Chimpanzee as Robbie Williams

Perhaps the most daring and talked-about aspect of Better Man was the decision to depict Robbie Williams as a CGI chimpanzee. This creative choice, inspired by Robbie's self-description of feeling "less evolved than other people," was both a metaphor and a narrative device. By presenting Robbie as a chimp, the film externalized his insecurities and self-doubt, making his internal struggles visible to the audience.

The decision to use cutting-edge CGI technology, executed by the renowned Wētā

FX, was integral to the success of this portrayal. Jonno Davies, a talented motion-capture artist, brought Robbie's chimpanzee form to life with remarkable nuance, capturing both the physicality and the emotional complexity of the character.

Robbie himself provided the voice, further blurring the lines between the man and his on-screen representation. This dual performance, complemented by Davies' voicing of Robbie's younger self, created a layered and poignant depiction of the pop star.

Crucially, the film treated the chimpanzee depiction as an unremarkable aspect of Robbie's world. No other characters commented on his appearance, reinforcing the idea that this was a reflection of Robbie's self-perception rather than an objective reality. This subtle narrative device allowed viewers to connect with Robbie's internal journey, encouraging empathy and understanding.

The use of a CGI chimpanzee also underscored the film's satirical tone. It poked fun at the conventions of biopics while inviting audiences to question their expectations of authenticity in storytelling. By embracing the absurd, Better Man achieved a unique balance of humor and pathos, capturing the essence of Robbie Williams in a way no traditional biopic could.

In sum, the introduction of Better Man sets the stage for a film that is as daring and unconventional as its subject. Michael Gracey's vision, the satirical narrative, and the groundbreaking choice of a CGI chimpanzee as Robbie Williams all combine to create a cinematic experience that redefines the boundaries of the musical biopic genre.

Through this lens, the story of Robbie Williams becomes not just a recounting of events but a profound exploration of identity, fame, and the human spirit.

CHAPTER ONE

The Idea Behind the Chimpanzee

At the heart of Better Man is Robbie Williams' deeply personal admission of feeling "less evolved than other people." This sentiment, which he openly shared during interviews, became the cornerstone of the film's most audacious creative choice: portraying Robbie as a chimpanzee. Far from a gimmick, this depiction encapsulated his internal struggles with self-worth, insecurity, and his often tumultuous relationship with fame.

The chimpanzee symbolizes Robbie's perception of himself as an outsider. While the world celebrated him as a larger-than-life pop icon, Robbie frequently grappled with feelings of inadequacy, a theme that runs throughout his career and personal life.

The film uses this animalistic representation to externalize these emotions, creating a visual metaphor that resonates with viewers. By embodying Robbie's sense of being "less evolved," the chimpanzee becomes a vessel for exploring his vulnerability and humanity.

Importantly, the choice also adds a layer of satire to the biopic. Biographical films often aim for hyper-realistic portrayals, but Better Man turns this convention on its head. The use of a CGI chimpanzee forces audiences to suspend their disbelief, focusing not on the physical representation but on the emotional truths of Robbie's story.

This bold artistic decision challenges viewers to confront the subjective nature of identity and self-perception, making the narrative deeply personal and universally relatable.

Designing the CGI Chimp: Behind the VFX Magic by Wētā FX

To bring Robbie's chimpanzee form to life, the filmmakers turned to Wētā FX, a world-renowned visual effects studio known for its groundbreaking work in films like The Lord of the Rings and Avatar. The task was as daunting as it was innovative: to create a CGI character that could convincingly capture the essence of Robbie

Williams while remaining visually distinct as a chimpanzee.

The process began with extensive research into chimpanzee anatomy and behavior. Wētā FX worked closely with motion-capture artists to study the nuances of movement, ensuring the CGI character felt authentic while retaining a stylized, human-like quality.

The design also incorporated subtle facial features and expressions inspired by Robbie himself. This fusion of realism and abstraction allowed the chimpanzee to serve as both a believable character and a symbolic extension of Robbie's psyche.

The attention to detail extended to the film's lighting, textures, and integration of the CGI chimp into live-action scenes. Wētā FX utilized state-of-the-art technology to ensure the chimpanzee interacted seamlessly with human characters and environments. Every hair, wrinkle, and gesture was meticulously crafted, creating a character that was both visually stunning and emotionally resonant.

Perhaps the most challenging aspect of the design was capturing the wide range of emotions that Robbie's character experiences throughout the film. From moments of joy and confidence to scenes of despair and self-doubt, the CGI chimpanzee needed to convey a depth of feeling that matched the complexity of the narrative.

Through advanced motion-capture technology and painstaking animation, Wētā FX succeeded in making the chimpanzee a fully realized and compelling representation of Robbie's inner world.

Jonno Davies and Robbie Williams: Collaboration in Motion Capture

The performance of Robbie's CGI chimpanzee was a collaborative effort between motion-capture artist Jonno Davies and Robbie Williams himself. Davies, known for his physicality and nuanced performances, was tasked with embodying the physical movements and expressions of the chimpanzee. Meanwhile, Robbie provided the voice and emotional framework for the character, infusing it with his trademark humor, charm, and vulnerability.

Davies approached the role with remarkable dedication. To prepare, he studied not only the physical behavior of chimpanzees but also Robbie's mannerisms, stage presence, and personality.

His performance needed to strike a delicate balance between animalistic authenticity and human relatability, a challenge he met with precision and creativity. Through motion capture, Davies brought a tactile realism to the character, ensuring that every movement felt natural and purposeful.

Robbie's involvement added another layer of authenticity. By voicing the character, he brought his own experiences and emotions to the role, creating a performance that was deeply personal. The decision to have Davies also voice Robbie's younger self further emphasized the thematic interplay between past and present, reinforcing the film's exploration of identity and growth.

The collaboration between Davies and Robbie extended beyond the technical aspects of the performance. The two worked closely with Michael Gracey and the creative team to ensure the character's portrayal aligned with the film's vision. This partnership was crucial in crafting a character that was not only visually and emotionally compelling but also true to Robbie's essence.

Overall, the chimpanzee portrayal of Robbie Williams stands as a testament to the power of collaboration and innovation. Through the combined efforts of Wētā FX, Jonno Davies, and Robbie Williams, Better Man transformed a bold artistic concept into a cinematic triumph, redefining what a biopic can be.

CHAPTER TWO

Early Life in Stoke-on-Trent

Robbie Williams' early years in Stoke-on-Trent were marked by formative experiences that left an indelible imprint on his psyche. Growing up in a working-class neighborhood, he faced the kind of everyday challenges that would later fuel his artistry. One such pivotal moment came on a football field, a scene vividly dramatized in Better Man.

In the film, eight-year-old Robbie is humiliated during a neighborhood football game when a failed attempt at scoring leads to mockery from his peers. The incident leaves him devastated, symbolizing the early seeds of insecurity and self-doubt that would plague him in later years.

The scene captures young Robbie storming off in tears, his small frame hunched with frustration and shame, an image that resonates with anyone who has ever felt the sting of public failure.

This episode serves as a microcosm of Robbie's lifelong struggle with self-esteem. While the ridicule of his peers may seem minor in hindsight, for a sensitive child, it reinforced feelings of inadequacy.

Robbie later admitted that such moments shaped his understanding of success and failure, planting the idea that he needed to prove his worth to those who doubted him.

In Better Man, this theme is revisited throughout his journey, where moments of triumph often follow deep-seated fears of inadequacy.

Family Dynamics: Betty's Support and Peter's Harshness

Family played a dual role in Robbie's formative years, providing both solace and strife. His grandmother, Betty, became a bedrock of unconditional support, often serving as the emotional counterbalance to the harsher dynamics he experienced with his father, Peter.

In Better Man, Betty is portrayed by Alison Steadman with warmth and wisdom, embodying the kind of love and encouragement Robbie desperately needed as a child.

Betty's role extended beyond that of a caregiver; she became Robbie's confidante and cheerleader. In one touching scene, Betty consoles a tearful Robbie after the football field humiliation, assuring him that his worth isn't defined by the opinions of others.

She sees his potential long before anyone else does, encouraging him to embrace his creativity and unique talents. Her unwavering faith in him provides a much-needed refuge in an otherwise turbulent household.

Conversely, Robbie's relationship with his father, Peter, was far more complicated. Peter, a former nightclub singer, introduced Robbie to the world of performance, instilling in him a love for music and the stage.

However, his mentorship was often tinged with criticism and emotional distance. In the film, Peter is portrayed as a man torn between his own unrealized ambitions and the responsibility of nurturing his son's talents.

One poignant moment in Better Man shows Peter teaching Robbie to sing in a style inspired by Frank Sinatra. While the scene captures a rare moment of bonding, it also reveals Peter's exacting nature.

He corrects Robbie's every note, leaving the boy simultaneously inspired and defeated. Peter's absence during significant moments of Robbie's childhood, including his performances, further strained their relationship, creating a void that Robbie would carry into adulthood.

Robbie's First Stage Moment: A School Play Triumph

Despite the challenges he faced at home and on the playground, Robbie's innate theatrical talent began to shine through at an early age. His first taste of the stage came during a school play, a moment that would foreshadow his future as an entertainer. In Better Man, this scene is depicted with a mix of humor and poignancy, highlighting Robbie's natural charisma and resilience.

The play, a modest production at his local school, gave Robbie an opportunity to step into the spotlight for the first time. After an accident backstage—where he humorously recovers from a wardrobe malfunction—Robbie delivers a performance that captivates the audience. The cheers and laughter from his classmates and teachers fill him with a sense of belonging and purpose that he had rarely experienced before.

This triumph, however small, marked a turning point for young Robbie. It was a moment where he realized the power of performance not just as a means of expression but as a way to connect with others. In the film, this realization is visualized through a glowing spotlight that seems to envelop him, symbolizing his awakening to the magic of the stage.

However, the elation is short-lived. Upon returning home, Robbie finds that his father, Peter, is absent, having missed the performance entirely. The sting of this absence is palpable, adding a bittersweet undertone to what should have been a purely joyous memory. This juxtaposition of triumph and disappointment became a recurring theme in Robbie's life, shaping his drive to seek validation through his art.

Reflections on Early Life

The depiction of Robbie Williams' early life in Stoke-on-Trent is not just a recounting of childhood events but a deep dive into the origins of his insecurities, ambitions, and creative spirit. From the humiliation on the football field to the warmth of Betty's support and the bittersweet triumph of his first stage moment, these formative experiences laid the foundation for the man he would become.

By exploring these moments with nuance and empathy, Better Man paints a vivid portrait of a boy who dreamed big despite the obstacles in his path. These early years are more than just a prologue; they are the key to understanding the complexities of Robbie Williams as both a person and an artist.

CHAPTER THREE

The Formation of Take That

In 1990, a teenage Robbie Williams stumbled upon an audition notice that would forever alter the trajectory of his life. Living in Stoke-on-Trent with dreams of fame that felt impossibly distant, Robbie's leap of faith to audition for a Manchester-based boy band would mark the beginning of his meteoric rise.

In Better Man, this pivotal moment is dramatized with equal parts humor and poignancy, showcasing the determination and charisma that set Robbie apart from the start.

Initially, Robbie's audition was anything but smooth. Clad in an oversized tracksuit and exuding nervous energy, he was initially dismissed by Nigel Martin-Smith, the shrewd and calculating manager behind Take That.

However, Robbie's resilience and sheer confidence quickly won Nigel over. In one particularly memorable scene, Robbie cheekily performs a dance routine to show his flair, leaving Nigel both amused and impressed. It's a moment that encapsulates Robbie's audacity and charm—qualities that would define his career.

The film also highlights Robbie's youth compared to the other members of Take That. At just 16, he was the youngest in the group, making him an underdog from the start.

However, his energy and willingness to push boundaries made him stand out, even as he struggled to find his footing among the more seasoned performers. The audition scene underscores this dynamic, setting the stage for the tensions and triumphs that would characterize his time in the band.

Navigating the Seedy Beginnings: Performances in Gay Clubs

Before Take That became a household name, the band's early days were far from glamorous. With little money and an uncertain future, the group began performing in gay clubs across the UK—a far cry from the arenas and stadiums they would later fill. These gigs, though modest, were instrumental in shaping the band's dynamic and performance style.

In Better Man, these early performances are depicted with a mix of grit and humor. The film doesn't shy away from the uncomfortable realities of the era, portraying the band's initial discomfort with the venues while also celebrating the sense of community and acceptance they found there.

For Robbie, these performances were a crash course in resilience and adaptability. Despite their awkward beginnings, the band's growing confidence and connection with audiences began to emerge during these shows.

One particularly striking scene shows Take That performing an energetic routine to a sparse but enthusiastic crowd. The cramped stage, flashing neon lights, and roaring approval from the audience capture the raw, unpolished charm of these early days. Robbie, portrayed as both eager and self-conscious, begins to experiment with his stage presence, laying the groundwork for the captivating performer he would later become.

These experiences also introduced the band to the realities of the entertainment industry. The pressure to conform, the financial struggles, and the need to constantly prove themselves were all lessons learned during these formative gigs.

For Robbie, the exposure to diverse audiences and the freedom to push boundaries would leave a lasting impact on his approach to music and performance.

The Explosion of Fame: Winning Teenage Hearts

Take That's journey from obscure beginnings to pop superstardom is one of the defining arcs of Robbie's career. As the band refined their sound and image, their fanbase grew exponentially, culminating in a frenzy of teenage adoration that catapulted them into the spotlight. For Robbie, this newfound fame was both exhilarating and overwhelming, a duality that Better Man explores in vivid detail.

The turning point comes during a pivotal performance in the film, where Take That plays to a packed crowd of teenage girls for the first time. The scene is electric, with screaming fans waving banners, flashing lights, and the palpable energy of a band on the cusp of greatness. Robbie, initially stunned by the reception, quickly leans into the adoration, delivering a performance brimming with confidence and charisma.

However, the film also delves into the darker side of fame. For Robbie, the adulation of fans couldn't mask the pressures of being thrust into the public eye at such a young age. The relentless schedule, media scrutiny, and expectations of perfection began to take their toll.

In one poignant scene, Robbie retreats backstage after a concert, overwhelmed by the demands of his newfound celebrity. His isolation and self-doubt contrast starkly with the euphoric energy of the performance, highlighting the emotional cost of fame.

Take That's rise also brought creative tensions within the group, particularly between Robbie and Nigel Martin-Smith. As the band's success grew, so did Robbie's desire for creative freedom—a desire that often clashed with Nigel's vision for the group. These tensions would later play a significant role in Robbie's departure from the band, but in their early days, they were overshadowed by the sheer joy of their shared success.

Reflections on the Formation of Take That

The formation of Take That represents a transformative chapter in Robbie Williams' life. It was a period of discovery, growth, and unprecedented success, but it was also fraught with challenges and compromises.

In Better Man, this chapter is brought to life with a balance of humor, heart, and unflinching honesty. From the nerve-wracking audition to the gritty performances in gay clubs and the euphoric explosion of fame, these moments capture the complexity of Robbie's journey.

Through it all, the film highlights the duality of Robbie's experience: the thrill of achieving his dreams and the inner struggles that accompanied his rise. As he navigates the highs and lows of fame, the seeds of his future conflicts—and triumphs—are sown, setting the stage for the next chapter of his extraordinary story.

CHAPTER FOUR

The Struggles of Stardom

As Take That climbed the heights of global success, Robbie Williams began to face the darker undercurrents of fame. While his boyish charm and magnetic stage presence endeared him to millions of fans, behind the scenes, he was grappling with crippling self-doubt. This internal conflict, compounded by the relentless demands of stardom, marked the beginning of a downward spiral into substance abuse.

In Better Man, Robbie's struggles are portrayed with raw honesty, pulling back the curtain on the pressures of life as the youngest member of one of the most famous boy bands in the world.

In a particularly poignant scene, Robbie is seen backstage after a triumphant performance, his face a mix of exhaustion and unease. Despite the deafening applause of adoring fans, he retreats to his dressing room, where he numbs his insecurities with alcohol and pills.

The film doesn't shy away from depicting the toll that fame took on Robbie's mental health. Through a series of flashbacks and hallucinations, the audience is given a window into his fractured state of mind. Robbie begins to envision versions of himself—mocking, accusing, and doubting his every move. These manifestations symbolize his deep-seated feelings of inadequacy and his constant fear of failure.

Robbie's substance abuse escalates as he attempts to escape these inner demons. The camaraderie of the band provides some solace, but it is ultimately insufficient to counteract his growing dependence on drugs and alcohol.

In one harrowing scene, Robbie collapses in a hotel room after a night of partying, his isolation and despair starkly contrasting the glamorous public image of a pop star. This moment underscores the fragile line between success and self-destruction, a theme that resonates throughout Better Man.

Creative Clashes with Nigel Martin-Smith

While battling his inner demons, Robbie also found himself at odds with Nigel Martin-Smith, the meticulous and controlling manager of Take That. Nigel, portrayed in Better Man by Damon Herriman, is depicted as a savvy yet unyielding figure whose vision for the band often clashed with Robbie's creative aspirations.

As the youngest member of Take That, Robbie initially deferred to Nigel's authority. However, as the band's success grew, so did Robbie's desire for creative freedom.

He began to chafe against the strict image and formulaic routines imposed by Nigel, yearning for an opportunity to express himself authentically. These tensions are explored in several key scenes, where Robbie's frustration boils over during rehearsals and recording sessions.

One memorable confrontation occurs during the recording of a music video. Robbie suggests a more daring and unconventional approach, only to be dismissed by Nigel, who insists on sticking to the tried-and-true formula that had brought the band success. Robbie's resentment is palpable as he storms off the set, a symbolic moment that foreshadows his eventual departure from the group.

Nigel's focus on maintaining the band's wholesome image also clashed with Robbie's increasingly rebellious behavior. His antics, both on and off stage, became a source of tension within the group, with Nigel often stepping in to reprimand him.

In Better Man, these moments are portrayed with a mix of humor and gravity, highlighting the widening gap between Robbie's ambitions and the constraints of his role in Take That.

The Breaking Point: Departure from Take That

Robbie's departure from Take That was both inevitable and explosive. By 1995, tensions within the band had reached a boiling point, fueled by creative disagreements, Robbie's erratic behavior, and his escalating substance abuse. The breaking point came during a fateful meeting at Gary Barlow's mansion, where Robbie was confronted by his bandmates and Nigel.

In Better Man, this scene is depicted with high emotional stakes. The band gathers in a lavish yet somber setting, their faces a mix of concern and frustration. Robbie, visibly defensive and agitated, is cornered about his behavior and its impact on the group.

The confrontation is intense, with emotions running high as accusations and recriminations fly. Robbie's isolation becomes painfully clear as he realizes that the bond he once shared with his bandmates has eroded beyond repair.

When Nigel delivers the final ultimatum—conform or leave—Robbie's defiance takes center stage. In a moment of both liberation and despair, he chooses to walk away, knowing full well the risks involved. As he exits the mansion, the camera lingers on his solitary figure, capturing the bittersweet mix of freedom and uncertainty that defined this pivotal moment in his life.

Robbie's departure marked the end of an era for Take That and the beginning of an uncertain journey for him as a solo artist. In the immediate aftermath, he spiraled further into addiction and self-destructive behavior, haunted by doubts about whether he could succeed on his own.

However, this turning point also set the stage for his eventual reinvention and redemption, themes that are explored in later chapters of Better Man.

Reflections on the Struggles of Stardom

The struggles Robbie Williams faced during his time with Take That serve as a stark reminder of the hidden costs of fame. Beneath the glitz and glamour of pop stardom lay a world of intense pressure, personal conflict, and emotional turmoil.

Through its unflinching portrayal of Robbie's inner battles, Better Man sheds light on the complexities of his journey, offering a nuanced and empathetic perspective on the challenges he faced.

From the depths of self-doubt and addiction to the creative clashes that ultimately led to his departure, this chapter captures the fragility and resilience of a young man thrust into the spotlight too soon. Robbie's struggles may have nearly consumed him, but they also fueled his determination to carve out his own path, setting the stage for the next phase of his extraordinary life.

CHAPTER FIVE

Solo Stardom and Redemption

After leaving Take That in 1995, Robbie Williams faced an uncertain future. The world watched with skepticism as the youngest and most volatile member of the wildly successful boyband attempted to strike out on his own.

While his departure from the band had freed him creatively, it left him floundering without direction. Enter Guy Chambers, the songwriter and producer who would become instrumental in Robbie's transformation into a solo superstar.

In Better Man, the partnership between Robbie and Guy is depicted as a serendipitous meeting of minds. Guy, played with understated charm by Tom Budge, is introduced as a talented yet underappreciated musician.

Their initial meeting, staged in a modest recording studio, brims with tension and potential. Robbie, still reeling from his departure from Take That, arrives late and unprepared, while Guy is skeptical about working with a "pop star" whose reputation for excess precedes him.

However, as the two begin to collaborate, their chemistry becomes undeniable. In a pivotal scene, Guy sits at the piano, playing the opening chords of what would become one of Robbie's most iconic songs.

Robbie, hesitant at first, begins to sing, his voice raw and vulnerable. The moment captures the essence of their partnership: a blending of Guy's musical sophistication and Robbie's emotional authenticity.

Their collaboration not only redefined Robbie's sound but also reignited his passion for music. Together, they crafted a series of songs that showcased his growth as an artist and a person.

Tracks like "Let Me Entertain You" and "Millennium" reflected Robbie's flamboyant energy, while more introspective songs like "No Regrets" revealed his emotional depth. Guy's guidance and belief in Robbie's potential proved to be the anchor he desperately needed, setting the stage for his triumphant return to the spotlight.

The Release of "Angels": A Career-Defining Moment

If there is a single moment that defines Robbie Williams' journey from boyband exile to global icon, it is the release of "Angels" in 1997.

Written by Robbie and Guy Chambers, the song became a cultural phenomenon, cementing his status as one of the UK's most beloved solo artists. In Better Man, the creation and impact of "Angels" are given a cinematic treatment befitting its legendary status.

The film dramatizes the writing of "Angels" as a deeply personal and cathartic process for Robbie. Struggling with feelings of isolation and longing for connection, he pours his heart into the lyrics, drawing inspiration from his own experiences and emotions.

Guy, recognizing the song's potential, helps Robbie shape it into a timeless ballad. In a powerful montage, we see the duo working tirelessly in the studio, their determination mirrored by flashes of Robbie's past struggles and triumphs.

The release of "Angels" is depicted as a watershed moment. The film captures the emotional intensity of Robbie's first live performance of the song, showing him visibly moved as the audience responds with overwhelming enthusiasm.

The sequence cuts between Robbie on stage and the reactions of fans from all walks of life, underscoring the song's universal appeal.

"Angels" not only revived Robbie's career but also solidified his identity as a solo artist. The song's success marked a turning point, silencing critics who had doubted his ability to thrive outside of Take That. More importantly, it gave Robbie a sense of purpose and validation, proving that he could connect with audiences on his own terms.

Personal Turmoil: Rocky Relationships and Losses

While Robbie's professional life soared, his personal life remained tumultuous. Better Man delves into the complexities of his relationships, portraying them as both a source of joy and a cause of heartache.

Central to this chapter is Robbie's romance with Nicole Appleton, a member of the girl group All Saints. Played by Raechelle Banno, Nicole is portrayed as a spirited and loving partner who struggles to navigate the challenges of dating a global superstar.

The film explores the highs and lows of their relationship, from carefree moments of happiness to heated arguments fueled by Robbie's insecurities and substance abuse.

In one particularly emotional scene, Nicole confronts Robbie about his self-destructive behavior, urging him to seek help. Her unwavering support serves as a reminder of the love and stability Robbie yearns for, even as his demons threaten to push her away.

Tragedy also strikes during this period with the death of Robbie's beloved grandmother, Betty. Played with warmth and wisdom by Alison Steadman, Betty is a constant source of comfort and guidance for Robbie throughout his life. Her passing leaves him devastated, compounding his struggles with grief and addiction.

In a poignant sequence, Robbie visits her grave, grappling with feelings of guilt and regret. The scene is accompanied by a haunting rendition of "She's the One," a song that becomes a tribute to Betty's enduring influence on his life.

Despite these personal setbacks, Robbie begins to take steps toward healing. The film portrays his decision to enter rehab as a pivotal moment of self-awareness and courage. Through a montage of therapy sessions and soul-searching, Robbie confronts the pain and insecurities that have plagued him for years.

This journey of redemption is not without its challenges, but it marks the beginning of a new chapter in his life—one defined by resilience and self-acceptance.

Reflections on Solo Stardom and Redemption

Overall, this chapter captures the duality of Robbie Williams' solo career: the soaring highs of artistic achievement and the crushing lows of personal turmoil. Through his partnership with Guy Chambers and the release of "Angels," Robbie found a voice that resonated with millions, proving his critics wrong and redefining his legacy.

At the same time, his struggles with relationships and loss serve as a reminder of the vulnerabilities that come with fame. Better Man presents these challenges with honesty and empathy, celebrating Robbie's resilience while acknowledging the complexities of his journey.

The chapter not only highlights his growth as an artist but also sets the stage for his ongoing quest for balance, purpose, and redemption.

CHAPTER SIX

The Knebworth Confrontation

The Knebworth concert in 2003 stands as one of the defining moments in Robbie Williams' career, both a triumph of his success and an overwhelming burden of expectations. In Better Man, this iconic performance is portrayed as the pinnacle of his ascent, but it is also a moment of crippling pressure and self-doubt.

The film captures Robbie preparing for the monumental show, facing the psychological weight of performing for 125,000 fans, a number that speaks to his immense popularity but also exacerbates his anxiety.

The film uses striking imagery to convey the overwhelming scale of the event. We see Robbie standing backstage, gazing out at the sea of fans, all eagerly awaiting his performance. The enormity of the crowd, paired with the deafening anticipation, makes Robbie feel both invincible and fragile.

The camera zooms in on his eyes, showing flashes of uncertainty. He isn't just performing for a crowd; he's performing to prove something—to himself, to his fans, and to the world. The expectations are not only external but deeply internal, a reflection of his desire to live up to the persona he has cultivated over the years.

The Knebworth sequence is juxtaposed with moments of introspection. As Robbie steps on stage, we are shown brief flashbacks to his earlier struggles, including his tumultuous exit from Take That, his battles with addiction, and his strained relationships.

These personal demons manifest in his mind, reminding him of the fragile foundations on which his fame rests. His performance becomes more than just a show—it's a test of his worth, and the weight of this test threatens to consume him.

Battling Demons: Hallucinations of the Past

As Robbie takes to the stage, the energy of the performance is electric, yet beneath the surface, a storm brews. In Better Man, Knebworth isn't just a concert—it becomes a battleground between Robbie and his inner demons. The film vividly depicts Robbie's mental struggle through a series of haunting hallucinations that plague him as he sings, blurring the lines between reality and his fractured psyche.

Throughout the performance, Robbie is haunted by images from his past. His father, Peter, looms over him in the shadows, an embodiment of the neglect and harshness that Robbie once endured. We see his younger self—unconfident and scared—reappearing on the stage beside him, a reflection of his unhealed wounds.

The hallucinations grow more intense as the show progresses, with the vision of his father morphing into other figures from his past—an amalgamation of his regrets, failures, and fears. These hallucinations are represented with surreal visual effects, where the lines between Robbie's reality and the distorted versions of his past blur.

The audience's adoration, captured in the loud cheers and applause, contrasts sharply with the emotional turmoil Robbie feels internally. The fanfare around him is like a cruel mirror, amplifying his self-doubt.

The film illustrates this psychological breakdown in a series of symbolic and disorienting shots—Robbie's body begins to contort, his voice warps, and the stadium becomes a chaotic blur. As his songs echo through the stadium, his inner voice grows louder, taunting him with past mistakes and insecurities.

One of the most powerful aspects of these hallucinations is how they show Robbie's battle not just with external expectations, but with the very image he has created of himself.

The larger-than-life persona that he has carefully built—his charisma, his confidence, his success—seems fragile when confronted by the haunting specters of his past. It's as if, in the face of such grandeur, he feels like an impostor, unable to reconcile the man he is with the man he once was.

The Symbolic Fight: Slaying Childhood Fears

The Knebworth performance reaches its climax in a deeply symbolic moment, where Robbie's battle with his past takes on a physical form. The hallucinations become an all-out psychological confrontation. Robbie, in the midst of his breakdown, is shown fighting off manifestations of his childhood fears—each one representing an emotional wound that has yet to heal.

In one of the film's most striking sequences, Robbie faces a younger version of himself, a scared and vulnerable child who once felt abandoned and unloved. The younger Robbie is portrayed as a more literal, yet deeply symbolic, version of himself—a reflection of the boy he once was, before fame, before success, before the overwhelming pressure of being someone he wasn't sure he wanted to be.

The image of this child represents Robbie's unresolved pain and his internalized sense of inferiority. In a surreal fight sequence, Robbie is seen battling this version of himself—angrily confronting the past that he has tried to outrun. The visuals are intense, with Robbie striking at the child version of himself in a way that almost feels like a violent purging of old trauma.

The film uses dramatic motion-capture effects to emphasize the intensity of the struggle, making it clear that this confrontation is both real and metaphorical.

It's as if Robbie is trying to free himself from the shackles of his childhood, attempting to overcome the fears that have always plagued him. This symbolic slaying of his younger self is not a literal act of violence but an emotional release—a moment of catharsis where Robbie finally confronts the child he once was and accepts the pain that comes with growing up.

This battle continues in the context of the concert, where the music itself serves as both a form of liberation and a vehicle for personal transformation. As Robbie fights his past, the chorus of "Angels" swells, representing his emotional release and a moment of transcendence. He overcomes his fear, and the hallucinations dissipate, replaced by clarity.

The roar of the crowd signifies that, despite the turmoil within him, he has emerged victorious—at least for now. It is a turning point, where Robbie begins to realize that his true battle is not with the external world but with the demons he has carried inside himself.

Overall, this chapter, centered on the Knebworth performance, encapsulates the crux of Better Man—a portrayal of the artist's journey not just through fame, but through the complexities of self-doubt, trauma, and personal growth. Robbie's struggle at Knebworth is not merely about performing in front of a massive crowd, but about facing the overwhelming weight of expectations and the scars of his past, ultimately emerging stronger in the process.

CHAPTER SEVEN

The Road to Recovery

After the emotional and psychological turmoil of the Knebworth concert, Better Man transitions into a pivotal phase of Robbie Williams' life: his journey into rehab and his battle against addiction. This chapter is one of the most poignant and raw in the film, showing the painful but necessary steps Robbie takes toward recovery.

The depiction of Robbie's entry into rehab is not one of simple redemption but one that is fraught with difficulty, self-denial, and moments of profound vulnerability. The film highlights Robbie's deep internal struggle, capturing the sense of hopelessness he feels as he faces the truth about his addiction.

The scenes are framed with stark realism, showing Robbie in a clinical, emotionless rehab facility—his surroundings cold, sterile, and unwelcoming. These early days are filled with painful withdrawal symptoms, uncomfortable group therapy sessions, and endless moments of introspection.

The film doesn't shy away from the ugly side of addiction, portraying Robbie as a man who, despite his fame and success, feels utterly lost and trapped within his own mind. The pressure to perform, to live up to an image that has long since ceased to reflect who he truly is, has worn him down.

He finds solace in a few unexpected places within the rehab facility, notably in his therapy sessions where he is forced to confront the truths he has spent years running from. In one particular sequence, Robbie sits through a support group where participants share their own stories of struggle.

He remains largely silent, retreating into himself, yet the scene is a turning point, symbolizing his reluctant acknowledgment of the need for change.

The portrayal of rehab in Better Man is not overly sentimental or sugarcoated—it's a grueling, emotional process, showing that recovery is not a linear path. Robbie's journey through rehab is mirrored with flashbacks to his past, linking his addiction to unresolved emotional wounds and deep-seated insecurities.

The physical and emotional toll of the process is depicted as excruciating, but it also marks the beginning of his transformation.

There is a quiet, cathartic moment in rehab when Robbie is finally able to shed his former persona, at least temporarily. As the film visually reinforces, his time in rehab represents a stripping away of the superficial layers of fame and expectation.

Robbie begins to understand that in order to recover, he must first shed the mask of the persona that has defined him for so long. The self-inflicted scars of his past begin to surface, but it's in this painful confrontation with himself that he begins to heal.

Rebuilding Connections: Family, Friends, and Forgiveness

A significant part of Robbie's recovery is rooted in his relationships with those closest to him—his family and friends. Better Man paints an emotional and touching portrait of Robbie's reconnection with his loved ones, showing that true healing requires not only self-acceptance but also the forgiveness and understanding of those he's hurt along the way.

The reconnection with his family is depicted with tenderness and sincerity, focusing on Robbie's evolving relationship with his estranged father, Peter. Their relationship has always been fraught with tension, largely due to Peter's harshness and neglect during Robbie's formative years.

In the film, Robbie's time in rehab becomes a catalyst for change, allowing him to approach his father with an open heart. The emotional reunion between father and son is understated but powerful—there are no grand speeches, only a simple acknowledgment of the pain and distance between them.

This moment of reconciliation is portrayed against the backdrop of their shared history, with Robbie recalling moments from his childhood that defined their relationship. Peter's absence during critical moments in Robbie's life weighs heavily on him, yet the film suggests that true healing comes through the vulnerability of forgiveness.

Robbie, now more self-aware, reaches out to his father not just to repair the damage but to understand the complexity of their bond. Peter, too, begins to show signs of remorse, and the father-son dynamic subtly shifts as both men begin to rebuild their fractured relationship.

Robbie also reaches out to his childhood friend, Nate, played by Frazer Hadfield, a figure who has long been absent from his life. The reunion is emotional, filled with nostalgia and a sense of lost time.

For Robbie, reconnecting with Nate is a return to a simpler, more authentic version of himself—the boy who had dreams before fame complicated everything. Nate's presence in the film is a reminder that even amidst the excesses of stardom, there is still value in the bonds formed before fame entered the picture.

In addition to mending relationships with family, Robbie must also reckon with his turbulent past with former partners, particularly Nicole Appleton. Their breakup is depicted with emotional weight, showing the toll it took on both of them.

Nicole's presence in Robbie's life is symbolic of his search for love and stability, but the fractured nature of their relationship mirrors his larger emotional struggles. However, in this period of recovery, Robbie learns that healing isn't just about making amends—it's about letting go of past attachments and forgiving himself for the mistakes he has made.

The film doesn't present a perfect resolution but highlights the gradual process of forgiveness and emotional rebuilding. In the end, Robbie's recovery is not just about overcoming addiction, but about mending the deep emotional fractures that have shaped his life.

Honoring Betty's Legacy: Finding Peace

One of the most profound emotional arcs in Better Man is Robbie's connection to his grandmother Betty, whose death has a lasting impact on him. Betty was one of the few people in Robbie's life who consistently showed him love and support, and her passing left a void that Robbie struggled to fill. In the film, Betty's memory is a constant presence in Robbie's journey, and her legacy becomes a key component of his road to recovery.

Robbie's return to Betty's grave is an emotional and symbolic moment of closure. It is here, at her resting place, that Robbie finds the peace he has been searching for. The film's portrayal of this scene is intimate and poignant, with Robbie standing silently at her grave, reflecting on the love and guidance she provided throughout his life.

This moment of reflection allows Robbie to acknowledge the emotional debt he owes to Betty for helping shape the person he became. It is through this act of remembering and honoring her that Robbie begins to accept the person he is, flaws and all.

The funeral sequence also underscores the theme of acceptance in the film. Robbie, still burdened with guilt and loss, finds solace not through grand gestures but through simple moments of reflection.

The film shows Robbie kneeling at Betty's grave, speaking softly to her, as if trying to make peace with his own self-doubt and guilt. The idea that Betty, in her quiet wisdom, would have accepted him for who he truly was becomes a powerful emotional anchor for Robbie's transformation.

This connection to Betty's legacy becomes a cornerstone for Robbie's personal growth. By embracing the love she gave him, he is able to confront the emotional chaos of his past and move forward with a renewed sense of purpose. It is through the memory of Betty and the reconciliation with his past that Robbie finally begins to reconcile his inner turmoil, finding peace and a sense of closure that had long eluded him.

CHAPTER EIGHT

The Triumph of the Royal Albert Hall

The climax of Better Man takes place during the Royal Albert Hall concert, a defining moment in Robbie Williams' journey of self-discovery and redemption. This chapter is a masterful blend of historical reconstruction and emotional catharsis, where the film culminates in a symbolic performance that represents Robbie's long road from self-doubt to self-acceptance.

The Royal Albert Hall concert scenes are not merely a recreation of a memorable musical performance but a visual and emotional crescendo that ties together Robbie's past struggles and his present triumphs.

The filmmakers took great care to reproduce the electrifying atmosphere of the live concert, capturing the grandeur of the venue and the raw energy of Robbie's performance in a way that emphasizes the stakes of this pivotal moment in the film.

However, what sets this sequence apart is how it integrates Robbie's inner turmoil into the live performance, blending the physical reality of his concert with the emotional and psychological battles he's facing within himself.

The concert scenes are interspersed with flashbacks to Robbie's tumultuous past, where the presence of his childhood self and other past versions of him looms large.

As Robbie steps onto the stage, the camera lingers on his face, showing both his anxiety and his resolve. The audience, unaware of the inner conflict he's experiencing, cheers in adulation, but for Robbie, this performance is far more than a public display of talent—it's a private confrontation with his own history.

The emotional intensity of the concert is heightened by the use of visual effects, seamlessly blending the real-world performance with metaphorical representations of his past, struggles, and victories.

In a surreal sequence, Robbie's past selves—his younger self, his addicted self, and the persona of "the bad boy"—manifest as figures on the periphery of the stage, watching him perform, taunting him, but also offering a kind of reflection. The performance at the Royal Albert Hall is both a literal and figurative stage for Robbie's battle to reconcile his various identities.

The audience in the film reacts to Robbie's music, but it's clear that this concert is as much for him as it is for them. The cathartic release he experiences during this performance is palpable, a moment of triumph as he overcomes the ghosts of his past.

The music is the emotional backbone of this chapter, with Robbie's renditions of his most iconic songs—the ones that defined his career—delivered with raw emotionality.

The performances are not simply about technical proficiency but about conveying the weight of a man who has been through the fire and emerged stronger. The use of songs like “Angels” and “Let Me Entertain You” gives the audience a sense of how Robbie’s music has served as both a coping mechanism and a tool for expression throughout his life.

Each note played on stage is charged with a deeper emotional significance, marking Robbie’s reclamation of his identity and his place in the world.

A Father-Son Reconciliation: "My Way" on Stage

Perhaps the most emotionally charged moment of the Royal Albert Hall performance is the father-son reconciliation scene, set against the backdrop of a rendition of Frank Sinatra's "My Way." This iconic song, famously associated with themes of regret, redemption, and personal reflection, becomes the vehicle for Robbie's long-overdue reconciliation with his father, Peter.

As Robbie performs "My Way," the weight of the lyrics is amplified by the deep emotional history between father and son. The scene is framed as a cathartic moment of understanding and healing. For years, Robbie had struggled with the harshness of his father's treatment and the absence of his emotional support.

But in this moment, as the song progresses, the tension between them slowly unravels. The camera cuts between Robbie's performance and his father in the audience, who, for the first time in the film, is shown with an expression of pride rather than disdain.

The inclusion of "My Way" serves as a powerful metaphor for Robbie's journey—he has lived his life on his own terms, but that independence has come at a great cost. Singing this song in front of his father is not just an artistic choice but a symbolic act of reconciliation.

As Robbie hits the poignant notes of the song, it's clear that he is acknowledging the pain of their past, but also offering his father a path toward understanding. It is a moment of catharsis for both men.

The performance of “My Way” is filled with quiet emotion. Robbie doesn’t sing it with the bombastic energy of some of his other songs; instead, he imbues it with a reflective sadness that matches the weight of his personal journey. The camera lingers on his face as he sings, showing the vulnerability that has come to define his recovery.

For Peter, this moment is transformative. The expression on his face changes from skepticism to something akin to respect and love—two emotions that have long been absent from their relationship. The camera moves back and forth between father and son, the space between them growing smaller, reflecting the emotional reconciliation taking place.

For Robbie, this scene marks the final step in healing the wounds caused by his father. The performance is not just a musical expression but an act of forgiveness, a surrendering of the anger that has clouded his judgment for so long.

By the end of the song, both Robbie and Peter seem to have shed the burdens of their past misunderstandings. It is a triumph not just of music but of the emotional maturity that comes with self-acceptance and growth.

Turning Pain into Purpose: Addressing the Younger Self

As Robbie reaches the pinnacle of his performance at the Royal Albert Hall, the final emotional layer of Better Man unfolds. It is during the song "My Way" that Robbie has his most powerful confrontation with his younger self, a moment that transcends the concert and enters the realm of self-empowerment.

In a powerful and surreal sequence, Robbie is confronted with visions of his younger self—representations of the child he once was, the troubled teenager, the lost boy of the past. These visions manifest as specters in the audience, haunting Robbie as he sings. Initially, the sight of his younger selves is disorienting and unsettling, yet as he continues to sing, something profound happens.

The vision of his younger self shifts from a source of shame to one of empowerment. The child he once was, who was bruised by rejection and weighed down by self-doubt, begins to smile, nodding in approval.

In this moment, Robbie's performance becomes more than just a show; it is an act of healing, a process of turning his pain into purpose. The younger version of himself, once a symbol of his deepest fears, now represents the growth and resilience he has cultivated over the years.

By singing directly to these visions of his past, Robbie is not only addressing the pain he once felt but transforming it into a source of personal strength. The moment serves as a metaphor for Robbie's overall transformation—he has made peace with his past and, in doing so, has found the purpose and clarity that had long eluded him.

The symbolic victory in this scene is potent: Robbie has not only conquered the demons of addiction and self-doubt but has also embraced the lessons of his past. The younger self no longer represents the victim of past trauma but a symbol of hope for the future.

In this climactic moment, Robbie's transformation is fully realized, and the concert becomes the culmination of his personal evolution—an acknowledgment of the battles he has fought and the man he has become.

Overall, the Royal Albert Hall concert scene in Better Man is more than just a performance; it is a moment of rebirth. Through his father's reconciliation, his acceptance of his past, and his triumphant connection with his younger self, Robbie Williams transforms from a man burdened by his past into one who is finally free to move forward.

The music, the stage, and the emotional catharsis all come together in a powerful moment of redemption, bringing the film to a heart-stirring, redemptive conclusion.

CHAPTER NINE

The Making of Better Man

The creation of Better Man was a monumental undertaking, requiring a harmonious blend of creativity, technology, and logistical coordination. Principal photography for the film took place at Docklands Studios Melbourne in 2022, where the heart of the film's production came to life. Filming in Melbourne provided the team with an opportunity to capture both the emotional depth and the fantastical elements of Robbie Williams' journey.

The decision to film in Docklands Studios was integral, as it provided the filmmakers with the vast soundstages and cutting-edge facilities required to bring the visual effects-heavy aspects of the film to life.

The team relied heavily on advanced motion capture technology and CGI, especially for the portrayal of Robbie as a chimpanzee, which was achieved through extensive VFX work by Wētā FX, one of the leading visual effects companies in the world. Docklands Studios served as the perfect base for creating these high-tech, immersive sequences.

Throughout filming, the production team meticulously built sets that replicated key moments of Robbie's life, from the smaller, more intimate scenes depicting his childhood struggles to the grandiose concert scenes that depict his rise to stardom.

The juxtaposition of these two extremes was critical to the film's ability to communicate the full scope of Robbie's emotional transformation. Filming was also intensive in terms of capturing the physicality of the performances, especially the live concert sequences.

Melbourne's studio environment offered more than just a controlled filming space—it allowed for collaboration between various departments, including VFX, cinematography, costume design, and sound, creating a cohesive vision for the project.

Director Michael Gracey and his team meticulously planned every scene, balancing the fantastical elements with the raw emotional moments that defined Robbie's life story.

The presence of advanced motion capture technology allowed for a highly collaborative environment between the filmmakers and Jonno Davies, who portrayed Robbie's CGI chimpanzee form.

The studio setting offered Davies the perfect space to bring his performance to life through motion capture, ensuring that the character was both technically proficient and emotionally compelling. The filming process at Docklands was as much about creative innovation as it was about capturing the raw, human essence of Robbie Williams' story.

The Role of Music: Re-sung Classics and Forbidden Road

The music of Better Man is not just a soundtrack—it is an essential part of the narrative itself. Robbie Williams' extensive catalog of hits, spanning his time with Take That and his solo career, was reworked and reinterpreted to suit the emotional arc of the film.

This re-singing of his most iconic tracks was a critical choice in crafting the film's tone, as the songs were not merely presented as they were originally performed but were given new emotional weight, aligning them with the film's satirical and dramatic themes.

One of the most significant challenges for the music team was to reinterpret Robbie's most popular songs so that they conveyed the emotional and psychological transformation of the character.

For example, “Angels” was not just a romantic anthem in Better Man—it was re-sung with a raw vulnerability that reflected Robbie’s internal struggles, infusing the song with a poignant, introspective quality.

The re-imagining of other classic hits, such as “Let Me Entertain You” and “She's the One,” served to reflect Robbie's shifting sense of self-worth, his battles with addiction, and his path toward redemption.

The film’s original score, composed by Batu Sener, complemented the re-sung classics by adding an atmospheric, emotive layer that enhanced the visual storytelling. Sener's compositions provided a musical backbone to the narrative, underscoring the intensity of Robbie's journey, from his darker, more chaotic moments to the hopeful crescendo of his Royal Albert Hall performance.

The score and re-sung songs blended seamlessly, ensuring that the music was both a reflection of the narrative and a force that propelled it forward.

Another crucial piece of the musical puzzle was the release of the song "Forbidden Road," which was created specifically for the film's soundtrack. This song encapsulates the themes of redemption and self-discovery central to the film.

Robbie Williams' emotional investment in the song, combined with his personal connection to the film, helped craft a track that spoke to his own struggles and triumphs.

Released in November 2024, "Forbidden Road" garnered immediate attention and was nominated for Best Original Song at the 82nd Golden Globe Awards. Its powerful melody and lyrical content made it a standout, and its inclusion in the film added an additional layer of emotional depth to the character's arc.

The significance of “Forbidden Road” extends beyond its role in the film itself. The song’s success, especially in the context of the film’s narrative, underscored the idea that Robbie had finally found his voice as an artist, both creatively and personally.

“Forbidden Road” was the perfect example of how music in Better Man was not just a soundtrack but an essential part of Robbie’s character evolution. Its success on the UK charts and its critical acclaim only amplified the emotional resonance of the film as a whole.

Bringing Vision to Life: The Creative Team and Cast

At the heart of Better Man's success lies the collaboration of a talented and diverse creative team, whose vision transformed the story of Robbie Williams into an emotionally rich, visually striking film. Director Michael Gracey, best known for his work on The Greatest Showman, brought his distinctive blend of spectacle and heart to the project.

Gracey's ability to balance humor, drama, and fantasy allowed Better Man to transcend the typical biographical narrative. He encouraged his actors to explore the emotional complexity of their characters while also embracing the more whimsical and surreal elements of the film, which were necessary to bring the concept of Robbie as a CGI chimpanzee to life.

The collaboration between Gracey, co-writers Oliver Cole and Simon Gleeson, and the film's producers was essential in shaping the tone and direction of the film. This creative team worked tirelessly to ensure that every scene, every line of dialogue, and every musical number felt purposeful and integral to the story.

From the visual aesthetic to the emotional beats, the team ensured that Better Man remained true to its unconventional premise while also capturing the emotional essence of Robbie Williams' journey.

The casting of Better Man was another critical element in bringing the story to life. Jonno Davies' performance as the CGI chimpanzee version of Robbie Williams was groundbreaking, as it combined motion capture technology with his ability to convey deep emotional nuance.

Davies’ collaboration with Robbie Williams, who voiced the adult Robbie, ensured that the character remained both fantastical and deeply human. Davies' portrayal of Robbie’s younger self, also done through motion capture, added an additional layer of depth, portraying Robbie’s inner child in a visually striking and emotionally resonant way.

Supporting actors like Steve Pemberton, Alison Steadman, and Kate Mulvany brought to life the key figures in Robbie’s life, imbuing their roles with authenticity and depth.

Pemberton's portrayal of Peter Williams, Robbie's father, was particularly noteworthy, as he balanced the role of a complex and often unsympathetic figure with moments of vulnerability that allowed the audience to understand the nuances of their difficult relationship.

Similarly, Steadman's portrayal of Betty, Robbie's grandmother, provided a steady emotional anchor for the character, emphasizing the importance of familial support during Robbie's darkest times.

The ensemble cast, including actors portraying the members of Take That, contributed to the film's authenticity, particularly in depicting the dynamic within the band during the tumultuous years of Robbie's career.

The performances of the cast were enhanced by the creative direction, which allowed them to embrace the larger-than-life nature of the film while remaining grounded in the raw emotion of Robbie's journey.

In addition to the actors, the creative team worked closely with the visual effects department, particularly Wētā FX, to ensure that the CGI chimpanzee version of Robbie was integrated seamlessly into the film. The VFX team, under the guidance of Gracey and the producers, was tasked with bringing a fully realized, emotionally expressive CGI character to the screen.

Through meticulous attention to detail, the team created a character that was both fantastical and relatable, making it possible for audiences to connect with Robbie in a way that was both unconventional and deeply impactful.

The collective efforts of the creative team, cast, and production staff came together to create a film that redefined the biographical genre, blending humor, fantasy, and heartfelt emotion in a way that had never been seen before. Each member of the team contributed their expertise, passion, and vision to ensure that Better Man was not just a film about Robbie Williams but an immersive, transformative cinematic experience that captured the essence of his life and art.

CHAPTER TEN

Reception and Legacy

Upon its release, Better Man quickly sparked intense discussions within the film industry, drawing praise and criticism for its bold reimagining of the traditional biographical formula.

Critics were particularly intrigued by the film's unconventional portrayal of Robbie Williams as a CGI chimpanzee, a narrative decision that could have seemed absurd in the wrong hands but was instead handled with emotional depth and creative flair.

On the review aggregator site Rotten Tomatoes, Better Man received glowing praise, with 90% of 94 critics' reviews being positive and an average rating of 7.5/10. Many reviewers were captivated by the film's audacity, with some referring to it as a groundbreaking, genre-defying masterpiece.

The satirical elements of the film were often noted for their wit and subversive take on the music biopic genre. The consensus on the site read: "Daring to substitute its marquee star with a VFX creation and somehow pulling it off, Better Man makes a monkey out of the traditional musical biopic to thrilling effect."

This unusual approach was seen as a refreshing departure from the often predictable formula of biographical films, which typically aim for realism and historical accuracy.

Metacritic, which assigns a weighted average score, also reflected the film's overall positive reception with a score of 78 out of 100, based on 30 critics' reviews. This score signified "generally favorable" reviews, with many critics praising the film's ability to balance humor, fantasy, and real-life drama.

The performance of Jonno Davies as the motion-captured Robbie Williams was a standout for many, with reviewers admiring his ability to capture the essence of Williams' character despite the CGI nature of his portrayal.

Audience reactions, however, were more mixed, particularly in the United States, where Williams has often struggled to achieve the level of fame enjoyed in the UK and Europe. American audiences found the satirical nature of the film to be a challenge, with some viewers unable to fully embrace the whimsical, surreal style of the narrative.

However, those familiar with Williams' work and his public persona found the film to be a deeply personal and moving exploration of his life. The film's success with international audiences contrasted with its more lukewarm reception in the U.S., highlighting the cultural divide in the perception of Williams himself.

Despite the polarized audience reception, the critical acclaim cemented Better Man as a striking, boundary-pushing piece of cinema, with its bold approach influencing the future of the biopic genre.

The film was celebrated for its innovative storytelling and its ability to both entertain and provoke thought, offering a new lens through which to view the life of one of pop music's most enigmatic figures.

Awards and Controversies: From AACTA Nominations to Oscar Drama

In addition to its critical reception, Better Man found recognition at prestigious award ceremonies, further establishing its place in cinematic history. The film earned a record-breaking 16 nominations at the 2025 AACTA Awards (Australian Academy of Cinema and Television Arts), making it one of the most-nominated films of the year.

These nominations spanned multiple categories, including Best Film, Best Director for Michael Gracey, Best Actor for Jonno Davies, and Best Original Score for Batu Sener. The sheer number of nominations indicated not only the film's critical success but also its wide-ranging appeal within the Australian film industry.

Better Man's success at the AACTA Awards highlighted its innovative storytelling and exceptional performances. The nominations were a testament to the film's boldness in reinterpreting the biographical genre while staying true to the emotional essence of Robbie Williams' life.

This recognition helped solidify the film as a cultural touchstone in Australia and boosted its visibility internationally, with many speculating that it would also dominate at other major award ceremonies.

However, the film's journey to the Oscars was not without controversy. One of the most significant issues that arose was the disqualification of the song "Forbidden Road," which had been shortlisted for the Academy Award for Best Original Song at the 97th Academy Awards.

Initially, the song was seen as a frontrunner for the prestigious honor, given its emotional resonance within the film and its popularity among audiences. However, a few days before the official Oscar nominations were announced, the Academy disqualified the song after it was found that the track incorporated elements from another existing composition, leading to a heated debate about originality and fair use in film music.

The controversy surrounding "Forbidden Road" sparked debates within the music and film industries about intellectual property, creative collaboration, and the ethical considerations of reworking and sampling existing musical material.

While the disqualification was a setback for the film, it did little to dampen its overall success, and the song remained a fan favorite, continuing to receive widespread airplay and praise for its emotional depth and connection to the themes of the film.

Despite this hiccup, Better Man garnered several other accolades and nominations, cementing its place as a film that dared to push boundaries.

The film's nominations at the Golden Globe Awards, including a nomination for “Forbidden Road” as Best Original Song, were a testament to its cultural significance and its ability to strike a chord with both critics and audiences.

The film’s multiple accolades and nominations proved that, despite the controversies, Better Man had successfully redefined expectations for biographical films.

Redefining Biopics: The Satirical and Musical Legacy

One of the most lasting legacies of Better Man is its role in redefining the biographical film genre. Traditionally, biopics have been known for their adherence to historical accuracy and their focus on portraying real-life figures with a sense of reverence.

Better Man, however, took a radically different approach by combining elements of satire, fantasy, and music to tell the story of Robbie Williams. This blend of genres allowed the film to transcend the traditional limitations of a biopic, resulting in a movie that felt both larger-than-life and deeply personal.

By using a CGI chimpanzee to represent Robbie Williams, the film invited audiences to see the artist through a new lens, one that was not confined by the typical visual representation of a celebrity but rather grounded in self-reflection, symbolism, and self-perception.

This unconventional portrayal was a bold commentary on how Williams himself viewed his place in the world, offering a unique interpretation of his struggles with fame, self-worth, and personal demons. The choice of using satire and visual effects allowed Better Man to comment on the often absurd nature of celebrity while still conveying a deeply human story of self-discovery and redemption.

Musically, Better Man also left a significant impact on the genre. The film's decision to re-sung Robbie Williams' greatest hits, reinterpreting them to fit the emotional arcs of the characters, elevated the songs beyond their original context.

These re-imagined versions of songs like "Angels" and "Let Me Entertain You" not only added emotional depth to the film but also opened a new chapter in the way music biopics can be approached.

Instead of merely showcasing a musician's hits, Better Man used music as a storytelling tool that deepened the emotional resonance of the narrative. The integration of original compositions like "Forbidden Road" demonstrated the film's innovative approach to music, making the soundtrack an integral part of the storytelling process.

In terms of legacy, Better Man has been hailed as a film that successfully deconstructed and reimagined the formulaic nature of the biopic genre. The use of satire, music, and fantastical elements in a biographical context created a new blueprint for future filmmakers who might seek to explore the lives of famous figures through unconventional lenses.

By tackling the life of Robbie Williams with a mix of humor, surrealism, and emotional depth, Better Man has become a symbol of how the biopic genre can evolve into something fresh and thought-provoking.

As a cultural artifact, Better Man continues to resonate with audiences, leaving an indelible mark on the world of film and music. It serves as a testament to the power of storytelling that transcends genre boundaries and highlights the importance of creativity and self-expression in all forms of art.

By reimagining Robbie Williams' life through a lens of self-perception and fantasy, Better Man has not only celebrated the complexity of its subject but also redefined what a biographical film can be.

CONCLUSION

Better Man's Bold Experiment: Challenging Biopic Conventions

Better Man stands as a trailblazing example of how the biopic genre can be redefined and reimagined for the modern age. By boldly defying expectations, the film presents a revolutionary departure from the formulaic structure typically found in biographical films.

In a genre often defined by straightforward depictions of famous figures, Better Man introduces elements of fantasy, satire, and surrealism, creating a cinematic experience that is as much about exploring the mind and emotions of its subject as it is about recounting his life story.

At the heart of Better Man's innovation lies its unconventional choice of portraying Robbie Williams as a CGI chimpanzee. This audacious decision disrupts the traditional biographical format, offering a metaphorical depiction of Williams' own self-perception.

Through this choice, the film opens a broader conversation about how biopics can move beyond simply presenting a linear recounting of events to exploring deeper themes of identity, mental health, self-worth, and the complexities of fame. The use of a VFX creation as the central character underscores the notion that the biopic genre doesn't have to be bound by realism to convey powerful emotional truths.

Furthermore, the film's satirical tone challenges the conventions of reverence often afforded to biographical subjects, offering an unflinching and occasionally humorous critique of the pressures of celebrity culture.

By mixing humor, fantasy, and raw emotional exploration, Better Man transforms the biopic into something both new and thought-provoking, showing that the genre can evolve into a space for artistic risk-taking and creative expression.

The way the film balances these elements—seriousness and absurdity, fantasy and reality—sets it apart from other films in the genre and ensures its place as an influential work of cinematic art.

In challenging biopic conventions, Better Man not only tells the story of Robbie Williams but also questions what it means to tell a life story on screen. It demonstrates that, in the right hands, a biographical narrative can be as imaginative and expansive as the subject's own experiences.

The film opens the door for other filmmakers to experiment with storytelling techniques, cinematic styles, and unconventional portrayals, offering a new roadmap for how to approach biographical filmmaking in the 21st century.

Robbie Williams' Legacy: A Journey of Growth and Entertainment

At its core, Better Man is a tribute to Robbie Williams' enduring legacy as a pop culture icon, but it is also a celebration of his personal growth, struggles, and eventual redemption. The film offers an intimate and often raw portrayal of Williams, capturing both the public and private aspects of his journey.

As a figure who has experienced both immense fame and significant personal challenges, Williams' life embodies the complex interplay of triumph and adversity that characterizes so many artistic careers. The film underscores the evolution of Williams, not just as a musician, but as a human being.

From his early struggles with self-esteem and rejection to his rise to fame and subsequent fall from grace, Better Man presents a portrait of a man who continually grapples with his own identity, the expectations placed on him, and the burdens of fame.

However, the narrative is ultimately one of redemption and reconciliation. The conclusion of the film, with Robbie Williams reconciling with his past selves and finding peace, represents a poignant and optimistic message about the power of personal growth, self-acceptance, and emotional healing.

Beyond the specifics of his career, the film also captures the universal themes of insecurity, ambition, addiction, and the search for meaning that many can relate to.

Williams' journey—marked by both immense success and painful lows—reflects the realities of being a public figure in the modern world, where the pressure to meet external expectations can often overshadow the pursuit of personal fulfillment.

In this sense, Better Man is not only a tribute to Williams' musical legacy but also an exploration of the complex relationship between public and private selves.

Through Better Man, audiences are reminded that Robbie Williams is more than just a pop star. His career, his struggles, and his journey toward self-improvement have shaped a lasting legacy, both as an entertainer and as a person who has openly navigated the ups and downs of life.

The film affirms that Williams' greatest achievement may not lie in his musical hits or fame, but in his resilience and his ability to confront his inner demons and transform them into sources of strength.

The Film's Place in History: A Symbol of Artistic Risk-Taking

Better Man will undoubtedly be remembered as a bold and daring artistic experiment that pushed the boundaries of what a biopic can be.

The film's audacity to blend satire, surrealism, and the traditional biographical format into a cohesive narrative is a testament to the creative vision of its director, Michael Gracey.

The project demonstrates the power of risk-taking in filmmaking and its potential to break free from the conventions that often limit creative expression.

In many ways, Better Man symbolizes the growing trend in cinema to embrace unconventional storytelling techniques. The decision to portray Robbie Williams as a CGI chimpanzee is just one example of how the film challenges viewers to think about biography, identity, and self-perception in ways that conventional biopics do not.

By using a fantastical visual representation, the film encourages audiences to look beyond the surface and engage with the deeper, often painful truths about the human condition, rather than merely accepting a glossy, idealized version of a celebrity's life.

Furthermore, the film's success highlights the increasing importance of creative collaboration in the modern filmmaking process. The merging of music, visual effects, and innovative storytelling not only elevates the emotional impact of the film but also redefines the role of music in biographical narratives.

The decision to reinterpret Williams' songs to suit the emotional beats of the story shows how music can be more than just a soundtrack— it can become an integral part of the narrative itself, further deepening the connection between the subject's life and the audience's experience.

In the long run, Better Man will be viewed as a turning point in the evolution of biographical filmmaking, especially in terms of its ability to blend fantasy, satire, and music. By taking artistic risks and challenging traditional storytelling norms, the film has paved the way for future projects that may seek to blend genres and explore the lives of famous individuals through more imaginative lenses.

The legacy of Better Man will extend beyond its critical and commercial success, influencing filmmakers, artists, and audiences alike. It has proven that even in an age of high-budget blockbusters and formulaic franchises, there is still room for artistic innovation and experimentation.

Better Man's place in film history is assured as a work that took risks, challenged conventions, and ultimately enriched the biopic genre by turning it into something both poignant and groundbreaking. Its legacy will inspire future filmmakers to continue pushing the boundaries of what cinema can achieve, making it a quintessential example of artistic risk-taking in the world of film.

THANKS FOR READING!!!

www.ingramcontent.com/pod-product-compliance
Ingram Content Group UK Ltd.
Pitfield, Milton Keynes, MK11 3LW, UK
UKHW020628290125
4342UKWH00044B/560